Tarik O'Regan

# LOVE RAISE YOUR VOICE

NOVELLO

Love raise your voice, Love sing your sweetest songs,
Love take the place where Death thinks he belongs.
Shady grove, my true love,
Shady grove I know,
I'm bound for the shady grove.
Love raise your voice, Love sing your sweetest songs,
Love take the place where Death thinks he belongs.

Andrew Motion

Andrew Motion hereby asserts his right to be identified as the author of the text in accordance with
Sections 77 & 78 of the Copyright Designs and Patents Act 1988.

**Duration**: *circa* 2 minutes

Order number: NOV959640
Also available for mezzo-soprano, baritone and piano: NOV958606

Novello & Company Limited
part of The Music Sales Group
14-15 Berners Street, London W1T 3LJ
Exclusive Distributors: Music Sales Limited
Newmarket Road, Bury St. Edmunds, Suffolk IP33 3YB
www.chesternovello.com
www.musicroom.com

# Love raise your voice

Andrew Motion

Tarik O'Regan
(b. 1978)

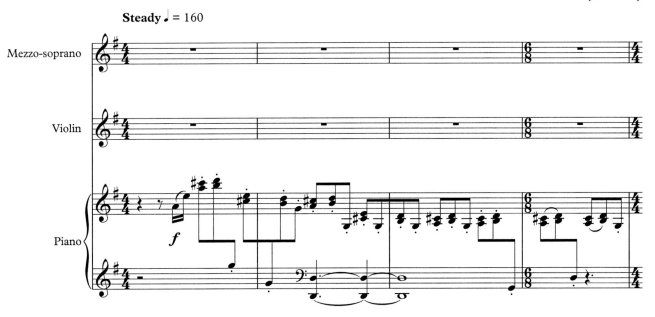

songs, Love take the place where Death thinks he be-longs. Oh,

Love___ raise your voice, Love___ sing your sweet-est___ songs,___ Love take

the place where Death thinks he be-longs. Oh, Love___ raise your voice,___

Love sing your sweet - est songs, Love take the place where__ Death thinks

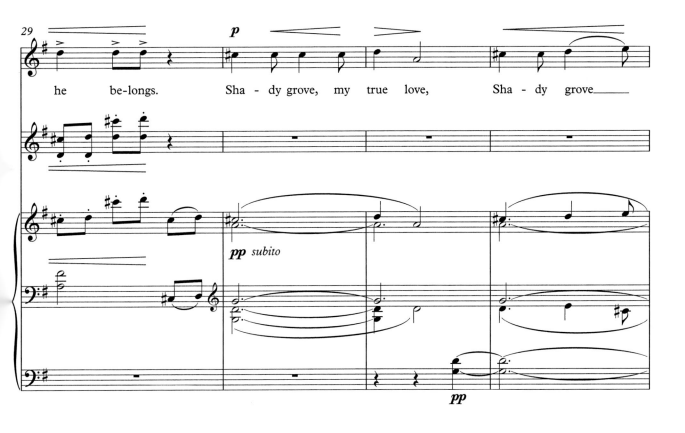

he be-longs. Sha - dy grove, my true love, Sha - dy grove__

Tarik O'Regan

# LOVE RAISE YOUR VOICE

for mezzo-soprano, violin and piano
(2009)

NOVELLO

# Love raise your voice

Violin

Tarik O'Regan
(b. 1978)

grove.

Oh,__ Love raise your voice,__ Love sing your sweet - est

songs, Love__ take__ the place_____ where Death__ thinks he be -

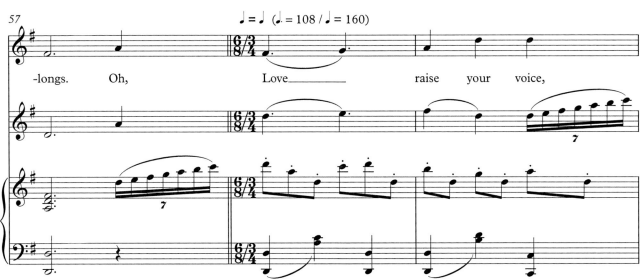

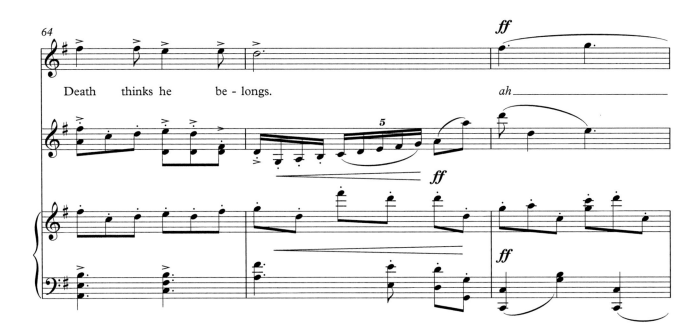

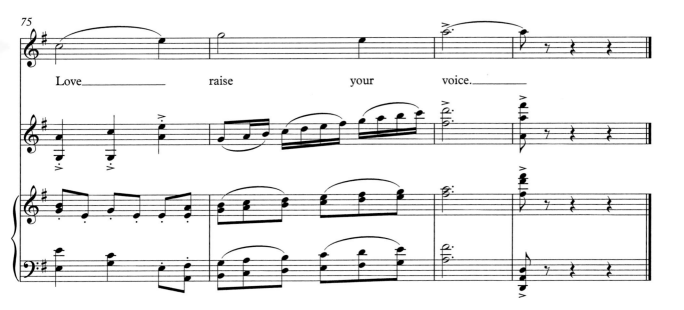